FOUND STYLE

FOUND STYLE

Vintage Ideas for Modern Living

David and Amy Butler

photographs by

Colin McGuire

CHRONICLE BOOKS

SAN FRANCISCO

Library of Congress Cataloging-in-Publication Data:
Butler, David.
Found style : vintage ideas for modern living / David and Amy Butler.
p. cm.
ISBN 0-8118-3673-8
1. Found objects (Art) in interior decoration. I. Butler, David. II. Title.
NK2115.5.F68 B88 2003
747—dc21
2002014613

Manufactured in China

Book Design by David Butler, Art of the Midwest Studio, LLC
Text by David and Amy Butler
Photographs by Colin McGuire
Art Direction and Styling by David and Amy Butler

Distributed in Canada by Raincoast Books
9050 Shaughnessy Street
Vancouver, British Columbia V6P 6E5

10 9 8 7 6 5 4 3 2 1

Chronicle Books LLC
85 Second Street
San Francisco, California 94105

www.chroniclebooks.com

CONTENTS

FINDING *YOUR* STYLE

Life is a process of continual discovery, and our surroundings should bear witness to the search. The best discoveries are those that are unique and exciting, with elements of the familiar and comforting. The same can be said for style, which can't be obtained by simply following a prescription. Good style is ultimately a found style—stumbled upon, discovered, and collected over time. It is easier to hire a designer, choose to be either shocking or conservative, to use massive clutter or leave rooms nearly empty for effect. But homes that feature a true sense of style are most often those that have been lovingly assembled over time, piece by piece, matching old and new with creativity, common sense, thriftiness, and occasional humor.

Found style has much to do with individual character. We all have our own unique sensibilities, but bringing these sensibilities to live in our homes requires going beyond established ideas of design, relying less heavily on retail giants, and exploring the vibrant consumer underworld. Flea markets, antique shops, swap meets, and garage sales offer items with character, culture, and history at affordable prices. The truth is, money can't buy style—only the appearance of taste—and adding character to your surroundings doesn't need to be a burden on the wallet.

Living creatively on a budget calls for innovation. For example, a fundamental aspect of found style is repurposing the old, using ordinary objects in unexpected ways to inspire a sense of delight. From vintage ice cube trays serving as desk organizers to surfboards acting as shelves, found objects say something about the finder and can be surprisingly functional as well. Repurposing is conservation at its best: beyond the obvious benefits of recycling, each vintage object possesses a story and a recollection of a different era.

The keys to found style are flexibility and function. Note that none of the homes in this book rely on a specific period or theme. Such rules would make it difficult for the owners to flex their creative muscles, to introduce a new piece here or there. The constant freedom to find objects and bring them home, and to adapt and adjust one's surroundings makes it possible to live creatively and comfortably. But have a credo: JUST BECAUSE YOU CAN DO SOMETHING DOESN'T MEAN YOU SHOULD. This refers to the particular habit we have of filling a room with cool finds from flea markets and sales simply because we like the objects. That's fine, as long as there is some form of restraint and voice. Ask yourself: Does this fit with the look I'm aiming for? Does it serve some (useful or other) purpose?

Artful accents. Boxes made from woven newspaper hold drawing supplies. The geometric patterns give their folk art roots a modern feeling. A vintage vanity mirror losing paint and silvering, is right at home amid shopworn apothecary jars and bottles. A casual smattering of greenery is easily changed for the whim of the day.

Style and function.
Years of collecting vintage
mirrors pays off with this
arrangement that not only
appears elegant but also serves
the practical purpose of pulling
light into a small stairway.
An industrial crate on wheels
has been given a second chance
as an artistic and sturdy chaise
with the addition of elegant
cushions and fabric. It's perfectly
suited for life in the loft.

Here is a set of found style guidelines to follow as closely or loosely as you see fit:

Use restraint with the objects of your desire. Editing is key to any well-conceived space. Hard-core collectors naturally want to surround themselves with their prizes, but please realize that your home can become a museum rather than a tribute to your passion. A wall of McCoy vases can be a beautiful addition to a room as long as the rest of the space is left for living. And don't be afraid to actually use the elements from your collections in your daily life.

Blend old and new. If your current collection leans toward the contemporary, the patina of a well-positioned vintage object can soften the look. An antique chair can be the perfect complement to a house full of modern pieces, lending context and history to the smooth lines and forms. Good design is timeless, and well-articulated rooms can combine vintage character with a contemporary format.

Create a keynote. For every room, determine the one thing in the space that will draw attention and set the tone. A wall of portraits? Architectural salvage? Period furniture? The room's color might be enough. With proper selection of the surrounding elements, it will be the one thing that people remember the most. Stylish rooms even tend to take on names reflecting their makeup (i.e.: the Mirror room or the Zen room).

Buy pieces with a purpose. When you're shopping the markets, shops, and sales, consider new and interesting uses for found objects. Think about how they will perform within a given space or if they'll serve multiple duties in various parts of your home. If they have a sense of purpose, it will make them that much more attractive. Of course, you'll still stumble on the occasional piece of sculpture or knickknack that serves no function but that you simply must have.

Don't fret. Great found style doesn't happen overnight. Don't become impatient waiting for your look to evolve. You'll end up falling back on a theme, or hiring a decorator, or buying the furnishings for an entire room at a department store—all sins in the world of personal voice and creativity! Allow yourself the time and energy to make something great for yourself. The process should be as fun and inventive as the end product. You will make mistakes, but in the end you will have a good sense of your own style and an organic space that changes with your whims.

CHAPTER 1

LIVING, BREATHING ROOMS

Whether we like it or not, our living rooms hold clues to our personalities and reflect where we are in our lives. Found style living rooms give insight while serving their primary purpose: comfort. Growing up, most people had the "good" living room and the television room, or family room. Many people still stick to this standard of having a beautifully decorated room that is seldom visited, as well as an area set aside for rumpus, disorganization, and relaxation—but the homes we feature here combine the two.

These homeowners let the stuffy, formal living room breathe by allowing the flotsam of daily life to intermingle with the cool, composed character of showy spaces. They tuck technology into vintage pine cupboards or display it sparingly. In essence, they've moved into the good living room and are actually *living* there. For many of us, there is no choice because we live in small spaces, or maybe we need a home office. Just remember that your rooms are to be lived in—the spaces (and their traditional uses) are part of a design challenge, not a barrier to good style.

Your rooms are part showcase for your design intuition, part theater for your family's daily drama. Use beautiful, found objects in serviceable and inventive ways. Hide speakers in woven baskets, corral remotes in a wooden box, and stow magazines in vintage suitcases behind the sofa. Allow quick cleanups of clutter by using old trays and picnic baskets to transport daily gear. If your space is small, think about investing in large floor pillows of vintage fabrics or old folding chairs for parties. Think ahead—these types of objects are often overlooked at the neighbor's garage sale and remembered in retrospect when needed.

Focal points. A small vessel in mercury glass calls attention with its graceful patina. A mid-twentieth-century worktable, cut down to coffee-table height, is given light and a new glass top to serve as the keynote design element in a simplified space. It becomes timeless, offering modern character with vintage roots, and anything placed on it becomes a work of art.

This brings us to the most attractive aspect of living spaces with good found style: change. We spend so much time in our homes that if we see room for improvement, we should be able to act upon it. With found style, it's not back to the department store to try and find bookshelves in the same finish as the rest of the furniture. Instead, it's about finding a more creative (and usually less expensive) alternative. If your purpose is to show off a growing book collection, then you might choose old steel-case file shelves or stacking oak cabinets. But if you want to simply tuck away clutter, a stack of old hatboxes might be all that is needed.

Remember, the key to a great living room is not so much what is in it, but rather how it makes you feel. Found style combines organization, comfort, and personal voice. It will invite friends and family in to relax, and make them feel special, maybe even honored, to be in the space. Your surroundings will tell a little bit about who you are—all you have to do is decide what you want that little bit to be.

Ideas and textures. Artwork weighing in as a family portrait under glass is held up by a simple flower frog. A classical, artistic touch is created by clustering formal china with a graceful bust and painting. A vintage safe acts as a very sturdy table between two leather club chairs. An oil drip pan from an automotive supply store becomes a waterproof tray for interior greenery atop an industrial green work table.

The essence of found style. An Adirondack rocker, a 1960s
Overman chair, a white marble kidney-shaped coffee table, and a
windmill; not the normal decorator mix. But with the right eye, good
editing, and a sense of form and detail, you can create a room that
invites conversation and a relaxed view. Chemistry beaker vases,
handmade pillows of vintage and new decorator fabrics, and a
mortar bowl full of eight balls are interesting and tactile conversation
starters that replace the remote control. A simple sprig of veronica
shows its artistic side resting in a lab beaker, and a 1950s
metal tray and stand make for an impromptu end table to hold
Asian-influenced collections amidst a sweet pea vine and dahlias.

Zen homestead. Modern sensibility meets Amish simplicity in a geometric display. A worn frame holds a well-preserved Amish portrait, seemingly akin to the girl on the opposite wall. The owners call the people in the portraits the "extended family," as they are always a topic of conversation. A small collection of heavy metal items sits atop a simple farm table awaiting use as wine caddy and ice service. A flat-back cabinet from the mid-1800s holds a tranquil collection of glass, a painting, a shell tree, and a vintage scale. Glass cloches cover the weighing plates, protecting heirloom portraits and letters. Old galvanized flower frogs prop up the images, and the entire ensemble tells a story. A large pine cupboard is just large enough to house an entertainment center and a collection of CDs and videos. The early twentieth-century work basket and baby bassinet on top of the cupboard hide the speakers.

Comfort found. A warm and tousled cottage is kept elegant through careful selection and sophisticated color. The turn-of-the-century wicker couch has been lovingly kept, and the cushions recovered in a rich, jewel-tone green to accent the warmth of the wood furnishings and floors. A built-in bureau holds tactile collections of paper, metal, and china that work together to create a focal vingnette. The fireplace and mantle no longer provide heat, but now offer stage presence for the stereo. The juxtaposition of old and new keeps the room rooted in the past, yet gives insight into the modern life of the family within.

Classic cool. An elegant space is made vibrant with the use of both modern and vintage touches. The beautiful, slightly worn Knoll coffee table seems to hold the room's focus with its slender base. It's also the perfect height for little ones to pull art supplies out and work on while watching the TV, which is hidden in the large, painted-oak cupboard. Anchored by Le Corbusier armchairs and hand-blown industrial task lights, the pieces were lovingly collected over the course of several years. The objects go together well; no individual item screams for all the attention. In the warm flow of materials and color in this room, note the hints of complementary blue that help add interest and support the use of cool metal end tables and lamps.

Warm and cool. A vintage metal hospital cart is all that is needed for holding candles and tucking away matches (and maybe the remote control). The industrial feel of the piece is tempered by the sophisticated collections and well-edited use of color throughout the room. Silhouettes, artistic glass grapes, an antique lamp, and transferware all coexist without detracting from each other.

Shades of light. The sophisticated use of color and texture is apparent in the combination of a well-worn cement plant stand, small vintage glass chandelier, and a painted tin candleholder. They stand alone as sculptural forms, but because of their style and color, go well together. As you begin to define your own style, you'll develop a vocabulary of form for yourself.

27.

Accenting comfort. Modern chairs intermingle with Knoll end tables from another era in a bay window that invites afternoon respites. A casual space like this calls for a kinetic design. A feather pillow of clear rip-stop nylon, made by an artisan, and newspaper boxes seem right at home amid the collection of family portraits and photographs. The room is a study in warm grays rather than harsh black and white.

Letting space dictate. In a converted social club, a young couple turned their found style loose on convention. Clean white walls, light-filled doorways, and a wide-open floor plan called out for a simple yet lively entertaining space. The floor itself has a great, subtle grid pattern left over from the torn-up linoleum tile. With two playful dogs, it's a stress-free finish that only gets better with time. Patina and sheen are carried throughout the space with the choice of contemporary furnishings and vintage accents. A touch of red in the pillows and artwork also helps pull the look together. A lightbox coffee table, converted from an industrial work station, acts as a centerpiece for the simply appointed room, while oversized seating pillows and a blond wood shelf (salvaged from a kitchen renovation) keep the mood as low-profile and cool as the Ducati 748 parked inside. Sketchbooks covered in vintage, hand-painted sign art create horizontal abstract art on a salvaged maple entertainment shelf.

Artistic expression. In a light-filled living room surrounded with art, found elements come into their own. Striking mid-century chairs found at an automobile dealership seem to stand out as sculpture; a dog figure bought in a Latvian antique shop rests upon a pile of flash cards, while grain silo vessels in salt-fired clay create a small cityscape. Sophisticated yet playful, this delicate blend of rural flavor and contemporary style honors the collection of stunning artwork. The combination of contemporary artwork and vintage furnishings become perfect conversation starters for the writer and the art historian who reside here.

Living with art.

Great found artwork isn't always easy to come by. And usually, when you do find something great at a flea market or shop, the seller knows it's great, too. Although some believe an artwork's value lies in its emotional attraction—or think that just because a piece is inexpensive it means it's not good—there aren't any rules regarding purchase price. Case in point, the etherial landscape at left was found for under $10 at a flea market. The unlikely duo beside it ended up together from entirely different folk roots, but feel right at home in their warm cove where they are allowed to shine. In a cooler setting not three feet from the folk characters, blue lead sculptures by Kristaps Gelzis of Latvia overshadow a flea-market head study in clay. They share the same stoic nature and sense of oblique humor as this lead pipe robot.

Many pieces of furniture that you will run into in your searches are considered to be high art in themselves. Do your homework if you want to become a collector. There are many reproductions, and a great deal of the classics are still in production today. A little knowledge goes a long way. The Bertoia-designed wire chair on page 2 was found at a roadside flea market for $150, a good deal on a classic that could fetch up to $900.

Relaxed reading. In the library, Le Corbusier's chaise lounge shares the room with a trash-rescued brocade beauty from the back alley. There is definite harmony in their setting, helped by color and texture that is carried right up to the beeswax wall sculptures in natural orange. Art in themselves, these wooden forms were once used to create molds for tractor engine parts.

Cottage life. The abundant use of warm and inviting textures help to give this well-lit small room a sense of familiarity while maintaining its clean, contemporary air. The leather of the vintage club chair acts as the perfect complement to the lighter matte finish of the overstuffed couch, and the 1800s shipping crate houses blankets for fireside evenings and trays for casual snacks. Light organza curtains made from yardage bought on a trip to New York are tacked up and pulled aside with casual fleetness and spontaneity. The complete absence of clutter makes for an easy change when the design bug bites. A collection of small bottles display natural treasures.

Symmetry. Occasionally, you will be inspired by one particular object and it may come to dictate the feeling for an entire room. Here, an early-twentieth-century walnut and oak side table shows a particular boldness in its symmetrical form and oversized pedestal supports. That flair is carried out in the classical chairs and the striking glass-tile candle sconces. The austere symmetry and bold contrasts are tempered by the soft greenery and delicate service pieces on the table. Vintage glass battery casings find new life as terrariums overgrowing with baby's tears. Items that might have simply ended up in a landfill now spark our imagination and continue to be useful.

41.

Displaying passion. In this sitting room, a series of show-dog portraits have been lovingly matted, framed, and hung with precision in a tight grid. This arrangement's scale and the close proximity of the pictures creates the feeling of one large work rather than a collection of small elements. Its detailed composition honors the subject matter and creates a warm, contemporary backdrop for humble, found-furniture pieces. The room carefully avoids the idea of a "theme" by allowing the collections to merely accent well-chosen colors and textures. The collection continues onto a painted wood coffee table, where a veritable dog park of folk art pieces romp and play.

Creating a cover. Great found style takes advantage of thrift and creativity, as shown here with a well-styled living space highlighted by slip-covered chairs and a sofa. When perfectly good furniture ceases to have the right color due to changing tastes, slipcovers can come into play. The room's cottage character is lightened with floor and ceiling colors that take advantage of natural light. To avoid an "all-white" antique feel, the couch was covered with gray upholstery-weight fabric and trimmed in black fringe piping that accents the black-framed artwork above. You can see here how well-edited collections add color and character without overwhelming a small space. In the opposite corner of the room sits an eclectic found-object clock created by the artisan owner. Made entirely of old wood, boxes, drawers, and hardware, it takes on the feeling of a family heirloom passed down from an eccentric relative—as, indeed, someday it will be. Vintage garden statuary collects light from the stained-glass window.

Found Space

This makeshift teepee becomes a brilliant vision in a sunny, formerly unused spot of the house. At the end of the stairwell, this space is too small for any "real" particular use. It could be left empty, a stubborn spot for a lonely chair or a catchall, but this unique child's play area takes on its own beautiful form when the morning light pours in. From a seemingly found space with simple materials—nothing more than canvas, a stapler, some twine, and dowels—a father created an adventurous retreat. Throw in some flea market satchels and a blanket or two, and play becomes art.

45.

Grand and humble entries. Occasionally, a space is so wonderful that you have to honor it. How you express yourself is ultimately a reflection of how you live. It can be hard to work with a large-scaled space, to fill it up or find massive furnishings that don't look miniaturized. This tile-floored entry hall in an 1830s mansion could be rather stuffy, but decorated with humility and grace, it now defines a living, breathing space. Not subject to being a display hall for a museum of furniture, it imparts a sense of activity and vibrancy. The impromptu cluster of garden topiary (resting on old grain driers) and a rare, vintage aluminum bike are all that is needed to create a sense of home in this large foyer. There's plenty of room for barefoot hide-and-seek, as Emma, seemingly out of the camera's eye, can attest. And in smaller spaces, wicker baskets for boots, or a simple mirror for catching a parting glance, reflect the same easy character.

In good form. Through the entryway and into the parlor, true found style makes itself at home, combining mid-twentieth-century furnishings with a simple pine coffee table and folk art dog centerpiece. Sophisticated juxtapositions create a sense of humor and individuality in a space that might otherwise prove to be uninviting. Instead, the forms and textures take on a sense of impromptu theater, creating a stage for everyday drama complete with red velvet curtains. Even in the most austere of spaces, there is room for humor. Painted yellow eyes lend a touch of whimsy to an otherwise serious dog sculpture.

CHAPTER 2

PUT TO WORK

No other space in the home reflects the found style impetus more than the creative work space or office. Maybe it's because such rooms seem to be pulled together from bits and pieces as we go along. Rarely is a home office pre-planned and formulated. Usually it's a quick fix, followed by an even quicker spreading brier patch of materials and technology. Even the space itself tends to be "found." We might commandeer a guest room or a corner of the living room; even a large closet can make do.

If living rooms are all about comfort and voice, creative work spaces are all about function and inspiration. They hold together your prime directive while allowing you to be yourself—something that doesn't happen as freely in the corporate office. For artists and writers, they can be as serene or as exciting as the work being created. For accountants and lawyers, they can pay tribute to a serious profession while lending a sense of humanity and personality. If you feel comfortable in your work space, so will everyone else, clients and family alike.

The functional aspects of a creative work space can be a form of self-expression. Old cigar boxes to hold desktop clutter, vintage mail sorters to hold stationery and supplies, and even the furniture can help to define a unique outlook. There is a feeling of reward when you find the perfect use for something otherwise useless or outdated—such as vintage suitcases stacked up to hold paperwork or compact discs.

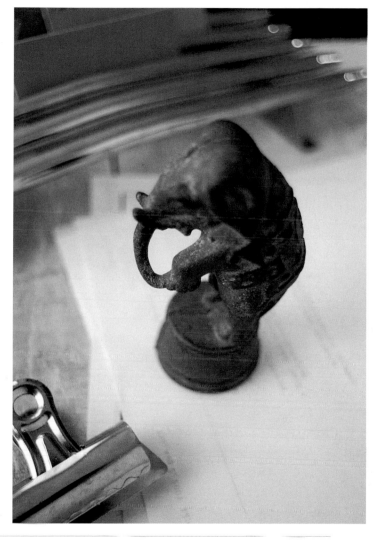

Creative combinations. Striking colors and juxtapositions do not necessarily have to be bold. The unusual can be just as dramatic without the inherent shock value. Here, a citrus-yellow Eames chair in fiberglass shares space with a painted canvas window cover in pastel mint. An old card file holds work supplies flanked by watering cans and old mirrors. If you found these objects in separate booths of a flea market, you might not think about placing them together. But with the kinetic approach of found style, trading furniture from room to room is how the best looks are created. An old circus elephant bank in cast metal becomes a great paperweight for the desk.

When you pull a new state-of-the-art laptop out and set it atop the patina and warmth of old wood amid vintage staplers and pens, it gives the impression of having values rooted in history while embracing the business needs of today. Going out and buying all new office furniture and storage bins can seem too much like an afterthought. With found style, you create the illusion that you've been doing your work for many years (even if you haven't), and that you're comfortable with your work. Trying to impose a corporate office look into your home can make the style appear forced.

Found style allows for easy growth and change. You can evolve your business and your look at the same time. Value and flexibility are reasons enough to embrace this movement! Your work space is very important, especially if you spend a large portion of your day there. It deserves the same passion for utility, style, and grace that you hold for the rest of your home.

Cool and composed. An assembly of boxes in complementary textures and colors combine to effectively organize clutter. A flower frog holds loose pencils, berry baskets collect flotsam, and an aluminum shipping case holds paperwork. A chromed piece of protective trim guard from a semi truck acts as the perfect desktop filing station.

Light industry. Work spaces revolve around work surfaces, and few command more authority than this industrial metal drafting table. For a product designer with limited space, a table and stool on wheels are the perfect centerpieces for various found storage units and shelving. The light and elegant space can be closed off from the main living area by two refitted French doors that hang on barn door slides. A hand-painted tapestry tempers light from a floor to ceiling window on the opposite wall, and vintage apothecary jars get their second life as models for new ideas and shapes. Our greatest steps forward usually find solid footing in the past.

Future present. A small corner office space takes
on a steely blue calm with the selective use of great
found objects and colors. The vintage medicine
cabinet shows off the usually mundane objects of the
day to-day office, giving them a sense of real impor
tance and honor. Stacking bins usually reserved for
the toolshed or barn hold supplies, and a simple
stretched wire holds clippings of inspiration. A love of
mechanical toys (and a little work-day humor) is given
a wink with this reproduction wind-up robot standing
guard in the cabinet, as well as the artistic winding
walker straddling the days mail.

Good thinking. For the corner office or pared-down think tank, you may need little more than laptop space and a few bill-paying supplies. Still, cool form can follow function with some unexpected twists using found objects and furniture. In this casual work space, worn painted finishes on a utility table show humble country character, while the angular shape of the weathered chair gives a modern flair. An alabaster table lamp sheds light on the drying rack in-box, and a 1950s ice-cube tray serves as desktop organizer. Betty the cat holds an impromptu meeting in the office on her 1960s rattan chair alongside an oblong wicker basket that used to carry mortar shells. The basket now serves a peaceful purpose as catch-all for miscellaneous office supplies. The pillow is of vintage bark cloth with new pom-pom fringe.

Details, details. Clever touches of pure form and pure function sit side by side on a work top. An old aluminum ice-cube tray has become the perfect desktop aid. Its $1 flea market price tag could never match its usefulness. Sometimes you have to look beyond the history of an item to see its potential. An outdoor lightbulb cover becomes a cloche to protect a family portrait held high by a music clip (from a marching-band instrument) lodged upright in a metal flower frog.

Collecting yourself. In an office corner, the perfect blend of passions rest on top of a cabinet, while overflow desk accessories hide below. The sculptural stacking of elements creates order and form in which nurtured plants become small trees set against a backdrop of ocher houses. There's no better place than the home office to find refuge for the passionate collections that inspire our work. In the open and airy space of this writer's nook, folk art portraits and sculptures of man's best friend dress up the old mail slot now in service of stationery and CD storage.

Guy style. In the writer's work space, wooden boxes and an old suitcase house dormant notes and manuscripts. The simple geometric forms and soothing colors reflect the organized calm of the space. Artwork and notes, too, are kept flexible and interchangeable to allow for fresh ideas. A system of found style boxes and drawers keeps clutter at bay. A jeweler's box holds the business at hand, while pint-sized dogs from the owner's collection adorn leather cubes full of staples and memo pads.

Clean living. This workstation is little more than a dedicated wall with a simple sideboard and chair. It offers enough room to catch the clutter of the day and tackle domestic paperwork. In an almost Shaker serenity, personality is achieved through choices. The use of contemporary task lighting keeps the space from becoming a museum, and the romance is kept pure by hiding obvious technology in satchels and under wool army blankets in wicker baskets.

67.

Creative multitasking. In this designer's studio, multiple projects are going on at once and the objects in the space are as creative and functional as the work at hand. A galvanized kitchen table acts as the main work surface, while a painted cedar chest, a wooden file set, and a mid-twentieth-century service cart all add their support. The entire space is developed from found style objects culled from various flea markets, shops, and antique malls. Hand-woven rugs add color and liven up the floor. Chairs have been brought in from industrial and educational auctions to supplement the idea that this is really a place for working. Gorgeous old cigar boxes and tins organize supplies while their colorful designs inspire. Transferware pitchers hold everything from knitting needles to paintbrushes. Instead of adding patterns or filling walls with pinup boards, simple backdrops in white and blue allow for small details to be noticed.

All in the presentation. Creating an aura about your work is important to keeping it fresh for yourself. Decorative "vignettes" are an inviting way to maintain the spirit of creativity that you seek every day, and they can be changed for new inspiration. A vintage dress form acts as an impromptu bag model in front of old letters taped to a wall, creating a scene of romance and subtle texture. A seat in the corner holds a tray full of details. A glass-top tea tray is only the first layer of beauty under flea market ceramic wares swimming in old glass beads. This "station" can be moved about the studio or house, chasing sunbeams. The value of a good tray with high sides and handles will usually far exceed its junk-store price tag.

Station to station

A kitchen service cart with cool lines
serves as a mobile home for trims and
fabrics. The easy-to-clean top acts as
an extended work surface while allowing the showy details to be clearly seen.
The trims and fabrics are all found
items; they will become beautiful
purses and bags in the hands of the
designer. Atop an aqua blue file
cabinet sits another tray station
awaiting attention with its project
inspiration tacked up behind. The
pin board is merely a piece of foam
core wrapped in a simple canvas
slipcover with a small handle. Multiple
boards lean against the walls awaiting
use, keeping the room free of clutter.

Wide open. In this painter's studio, a converted barn, found style supports the arts in the form of utilitarian palette holders, brush storage, and furnishings. Vintage garden end tables join a rough and extremely heavy industrial work stand in providing waist-high access to brushes and paints, while a slip-covered junk store chair provides the perfect place for review and contemplation. Because of the messy nature of painting large-scale oils, modest furnishings and recycled storage options are practical and sensible.

Painting retreat. In a smaller studio space, an artist has created a nook for relaxed watercolor studies. An old gardening bag and artist's box take the studio to the field or bring inspiration from nature back home. A potting bench proves to be the perfect height for detail paintings, and glass vases provide a clear view of just the right brush for the job. Found plant studies tacked to the wall provide inspiration, and a peacock-like sculpture of devil's claw seed pods makes for an interesting composition rendered in delicate lines.

Millinery at home. This artist's space, created entirely with found style, reflects the heritage of the hat-making craft. Using vintage hat forms and materials, the process itself harkens back to a more romantic era of fashion. Everything is kept close at hand: a general store shelf holds trimmings and details, vintage suitcases organize supplies and patterns, and a perimeter shelf displays hat blocks. An old shoe bag hangs beside the artist's chair to hold the most immediate and important items for the current task.

79.

Pure found style. Occasionally, the very impetus for producing art is the found material being used. For this hat maker, vintage and new trims, ribbons, and florets adorn her creations and are kept close by with the help of other found objects, as with these vintage wire racks. A cottage industry commands common sense and thrift, which can become part of the creative process and occasionally cause us to find beauty in unexpected places.

CHAPTER 3

TABLE MANNERS

The very idea of what a kitchen is and what a dining room is might seem quite disparate. But in the casual world of found style, they're more alike than different. If you're like us, while the eating may take place in the dining room, everything starts in the kitchen, including the entertaining. We spend a great deal of time in the kitchen, so it needs to be more than just utilitarian. And a well-appointed dining area should be as functional as it is beautiful. In both spaces, we break bread, share news, revive ourselves, and exchange ideas.

Food brings people together in the kitchen at all hours. It is a heavily used space that must also be appealing and even inspirational. Aspire to create a kitchen that is built for great cooking and spontaneous entertaining. It should be beautiful, practical, and tough. With clever uses of found objects like the ones you see here, you'll add layers of conversation to your culinary efforts.

Stainless-steel bins, industrial porcelain and milk-glass vessels, and restaurant shelving combine to create cool, easy-to-manage workstations. Airtight glass jars hold beans, flour, and rice in a practical and elegant manner. Old rolling carts make for flexible, space-saving

service or drink stations. For small kitchen spaces, look for creative vintage shelving or chimney cupboards to use as pantries between appliances.

Move that same spontaneity into the dining room. Beaker vases, vintage metal accents, and salvaged furniture combine to make a backdrop for an easy lunch or an elegant dinner. Look at how you want to use your dining room. If you see it as an extension of your kitchen, simply apply the same look. But when you want to treat friends or family to a formal meal, step up the elegance a few notches, at least temporarily.

Tactile beauty. In the clean lines and detailing of this vintage refrigerator door, you can see how, through found style, great art and craftsmanship are at your fingertips every day. A flea market farm table and painted chairs are the perfect size and character for this converted sun porch, with the kitchen just behind the large built-in island, gracefully moving from streamlined appliances to natural furnishings.

Too formal a dining room will go unused most of the time except on holidays and other special events—similar to the "good" living rooms we spoke of in chapter one.

Found style tends to eschew the traditional or overtly formal. Instead, it blends everyday living with the aesthetic of grace. Make loved ones feel honored and appreciated by inviting them into a world that you have created with passion and flair. The environment itself then becomes a part of the meal, a part of the story.

Glass light. Old glass pharmacy bottles set in the kitchen window awaiting duty as root starters for begonia cuttings. Fire King and blue glass take on diner-style charm when propped on genuine restaurant shelving. A dining room chandelier painted white is given an extra element of glitz with the addition of found crystals strung in a loose fashion.

Space savings. A small kitchen doesn't have to be a cramped galley, it just needs good planning and a few creative finds. Restaurant surplus is the key to making this small space work. Shelving and units designed to accommodate small commercial areas are just as practical at home. The industrial edge is tempered with the addition of glassware collections and cake stands nesting on a high perch. To make up for the absence of drawer space, this kitchen proudly displays cutlery and kitchen utensils in restaurant bins, galvanized buckets, and pitch pots, making for easy recognition and simple storage.

An elegant divide. Dining in elegance is made simple with a few found design notes. The formal dining area is divided from the kitchen table and work area by an impromptu scrim of light green hung in sections from a galvanized conduit pole. The space can be opened up or closed off depending on mood. A canvas tablecloth drops and gathers on the floor, while rose blossoms float in vintage ironstone.

Graceful display. A general-store flat back is more than large enough to hold all of the dinnerware and proves an elegant display for useful found collections. Although these well-positioned vignettes seem like studies in design, all of the items come out for use. This makes for lively and kinetic design as well, considering the elements will be arranged differently when they're put back in place.

Zen respite. This kitchen sitting area is little more than a spot for light lunching or reading the paper before garden work begins. A simple table for two and a few candelabras set a Zen-like stage for early morning meditation. Instead of cluttering the space with a table, sideboard, and chairs, the owners spent money on a large bank of French doors and allowed the room to breathe. A stainless-steel side table from auction holds water in such minimalist fashion that the very act of drinking it becomes a statement in pared-down living.

93.

Warm white. Rooms with great found style look like they've always been there. Using the visual cues of the home's interior, this dining room carries an unpretentious grace through the use of architectural salvage and family-worn furnishings. The large farm table is casually arranged with old ironstone pottery and glassware; nothing fussy or formal. It has the kind of patina and ease that invite family board games to take center stage.

Calm and collected. In a combination of deco diner and grandma's kitchen, this purely vintage kitchen takes on a contemporary character with the clean use of color and space. Vintage mirrors propped up behind the sink reflect natural light and help to keep an eye out for early dinner-party guests. An industrial shelving island holds milk crates, pharmaceutical files, and swimming pool locker baskets for keeping necessities close at hand, and a row of old mason jars hold the cooking basics on the reclaimed vintage formica counter.

The nook. Aluminum naval chairs flank a 1940s farm table in the kitchen corner, surrounded by window views out into the garden. Diner ware from a local grange act as everyday dishes, and plastic handled cutlery from a garage sale joins hydrangeas in old mason jars. White pumpkins sitting on old milk-glass cake stands, and treats served on a retro display are enticing accents. The practical addition of an insect screen gives it the feel of a 1950s bakery. A medical utensil tray with milk-glass inserts separates cutlery for quick grabs on the lunch counter. The wide-brimmed enamel light fixture hales from the musty basement of an antique store.

Green space. A cool palette of colors complements the warm character of the floor and helps tie together an amazing vocabulary of textures in this entertaining space. A primitive oak library table painted in white and surrounded by a hodgepodge of chairs in similar tones becomes the focal point for dining and conversation. Sheer white curtains hang from clips on simple wires strung from nail to nail. The tabletop displays a small collection of old crystal, metal service pieces, and glass cloches fitted to antique trays.

Bakery fresh. This baker's display case now serves as storage and a sideboard to show off the owner's collection of antique glassware. Inside the case, small displays of family portraiture mingle with mirrors and cut-crystal vases, inviting study and conversation. A small, rolling dentist's cabinet now acts as tableside bar service complete with found barware, shakers, silver-plated flutes and goblets, and even a handy dolphin bottle opener. Details from the corner tabletop show how the etchings in both metal and glass help to weave together a design story in small accents.

At the ready. With its absence of partition walls, this kitchen allows for active lifestyles and easy access to the living and dining rooms. Instead, a large island houses appliances and storage. Antique glassware helps to divide the rooms, but allows for light. Industrial restaurant shelving holds the kitchen utensils out in the open for easy access and the owner's spontaneous fits of baking. The yellow vintage fridge hails from the in-law's basement, where it has held leftovers for decades.

Many times you can find vintage refrigerators by asking appliance delivery men, who often haul out old refrigerators and take them to the dump. Bear in mind that the old condensers are not easily repaired, and the old freon style is no longer available.

Solid entertainment. This industrial worktable commands a certain amount of respect but not a great deal of pampering. Its patina takes on the character of soft suede under the warm glow of red candlelight and wood cabinetry. The symmetry of this simple dining room is its striking appeal. Mix-and-match office chairs found at auction and a painted-on area rug in deep vermilion hold their own under the giant steel tabletop.

CHAPTER 4

BEDDING DOWN

Serenity and calm are the keys to a successful bedroom space. For many people, the room is little more than a decompression chamber and changing station. But for those of us who spend a great deal of time in the bedroom, the need for a calm and collected space to unwind, meditate, and read motivates our design choices. The bedroom can become a mini retreat or hideaway that projects the peace of

mind we seek. After all, we need the reassurance of pleasant surroundings before drifting off to sleep and upon waking to a new morning. Seek simple, clean, light spaces that soothe without being stupefying. Avoid deep, chromatic tones and massive clutter, as these present challenge and anxiety—not things to deal with after a hard day.

The bedrooms shown in this book have been assembled by busy people with hectic lives. They reflect a beckoning call to slow down and breathe deep. Soft fabrics like chenille, light colors, Zen-like arrangements of mirrors or bottles, and images of pastoral tranquility are the prescription for self-preservation. Use found style to establish areas for vanity and relaxation, to make yourself feel pampered. Vintage glass for flowers, hooked rugs for cold feet at the bedside, and favorite works of art all have the same purposes in the bedroom: to calm and comfort.

Kids and teens, on the other hand, have a different set of parameters altogether. They spend more active time (and more time in general) in their rooms and so have other needs. Calm and cleanliness may be key for grown-ups, but privacy and self-expression are key for children. That's why we've taken a look at how found style might affect youngsters. For the very young, the bedroom is a safe haven of fantastic exploration and learning, as well as a protected fortress against the world at large. For the teen, the bedroom presents an opportunity for inspiration and creativity in a non-judgmental climate.

In charmed fashion. A white medical cabinet in the guest room holds overnight supplies for visitors. Folk art portraits combine with bucolic landscapes in the geometric play atop this bedroom fireplace, while simple twigs lie on the hearth. Vintage coverlets lie at the foot of the bed in anticipation of cool weather.

Having your kids decorate their rooms with found style is a great way to get them involved in learning about design and how it relates to their lives. Take them with you to flea markets and see what they enjoy. Guide them toward thinking about objects in functional and aesthetic ways. Remember that style can be a great reflection of desire. Just because your child is good at soccer now doesn't mean that they'll want to coat their room in it. They may grow bored with themed rooms quickly. Keep an open mind and understand that it's better to guide their approach rather than steer the boat. And, just maybe, they'll keep their rooms cleaner.

Storybook vanity. A wispy organza drape over the small table gives a Cinderella effect, while the vintage glass-door shelf above holds painted folk art birds reminiscent of storybook silhouettes. Along with the vintage table dressings and old mirrors, a youthful magic is created, just the right effect for primping.

Cool dreams. Bedrooms get much of their character from fabric. Continuing the sheer look here, a simple scrim attaches above the headboard and drapes to wrap around the end posts. Vintage ticking stripes adorn the newly constructed pillows that lie on top of the green-and-white chenille spread, and a wicker garden table acts as a foot chest for extra covers. Nightstands are also draped, to hide books and tissue boxes underneath. A family portrait exposes the relaxed character of the room as well as the family who resides here.

113.

Light sleeper. In this open space, the graceful dancing of subtle color and light is enhanced by collections of old glass bottles and mirrors. The elegant chandelier looks equally beautiful during the day hanging above the blank palette of the bed as it does dimly lit for nighttime reading. Here, the absence of pattern allows details to shine. A collection of small vanity mirrors act as a focal point above the bed, and small pharmacy bottles, when not holding sprigs of greenery or rooting divisions, are stored in the open as a small landscape of light.

Tuck in. Through color and patterning, an inviting comforter adds an exotic flair to this simply appointed room. Bright pink pillows in a floral pattern are another exclamation point to the light, cool hues of the walls and worn mirrors above. A brushed-metal end table acts as the perfect nightstand, and books have replaced tennis shoes in the old locker basket below. A reclaimed vanity has been sanded and coated to allow the old metal to shine through. Its enamel top remains intact. To soften its steely lines, paper lanterns and small, glass milk bottles highlight the surface, while foxglove stems rest in oversized vases on the floor.

The eyes of a child

Ordinary objects can become
magical when seen by a child. So can
spaces. Great kids' rooms give a
sense of invention and discovery—
and with a little help from the
grown-ups— will spark imagination
and sweet dreams. An elegant, old
ballerina dress complete with paper
flowers hangs waiting for just the
right girl with just the right
magic wand. In Jack's room,
fantasy has sprung up around the
bed in a halo arch of branches and
fairy lights. The small shades create
the perfect nightlight for studying
the giant castle, painted with
Mom's help.

Clubhouse life. This room could only have been created by someone who remembers what it's like to be a kid. Features include
pulleys to raise big windows (great for little hands), sailboat-style
bed curtains, a hideaway trundle for sleepovers and storage, and
a found-object astronaut to stand guard at night. A splash of cool
color raises big ideas at this little desk. All in all, a great place to
put up one's cowboy boots and dream of adventure.

MAX HELD

Pint-sized details. Childhood friends hang out in galvanized locker baskets, salvaged porch pieces hold up treasured toys, and a simple galvanized conduit supports sailboat-style curtains. A robot from outer space has a special place in the bedroom. Made of an old toy refrigerator with croquet mallet legs, he has a belly that opens wide to show his inner workings, and a helmet that comes off to expose a sly grin.

Design dude. Youthful design revolves around pulling together something cool with what you have. It's perfect found-style thinking, and in this case it's all about board riding. A surfboard perched on vintage speakers acts as shelving above the single bed. A collection of old skateboards and snowboards are "active" decorations alongside a 1970s horoscope clock and a set of mid-twentieth-century trophies (poking fun at traditional teen room dressing). A metal rolling cart carries an aluminum case full of CDs to neatly organize an audiophile's collection. A rustic bench and salvaged door act as gear storage and catchall for a once-uncontrollable pile.

125.

Girl power. A flexible, low-profile space is made exciting with the use of artwork and funky furniture. Using eclectic finds like an old mirror and chandelier, the corner primping station allows natural lighting and easy shifting. For an active girl who needs to flex out her small space for visiting friends, a normal bed just won't do. A roll pad takes on an Asian flair, with textiles, pillows, and throws neatly stacked beside an old silhouette and doll furniture. A 1960s hair dryer acts as a music station, while a life-sized portrait lets everybody know who the princess is in this pad. As the only object on the wall, it shows graceful restraint, a far cry from walls plastered with boy bands. Overstuffed floor pillows and stacks of magazines are all a girl needs, aside from her vanity, of course.

CHAPTER 5

WASHING UP

Washrooms share a common purpose, but their approach toward that dutiful end is based on the style and function we give them. They can be utilitarian or romantic, relaxing or cheerful. What is important is that the elements and materials you choose are relatively low-maintenance. The room is high in humidity, so avoid metals that rust, and raw paperboards and old woods that might mold. Look for heavy milk-glass jars, aluminum baskets, restaurant and medical supply containers, and other pieces that will maximize the efficiency of your space with flair.

What the washroom affords us, maybe more than anything else, is retreat. It is a place where we take care of ourselves; in essence, it is the fortress of our well-being. So in the time we spend there, we should be able to breathe deeply and take in the beauty of details. Pampering yourself with the calm presence of vintage pieces is relaxing and therapeutic in and of itself. Whether you indulge in a long bath in a claw-foot tub or a vigorous water massage in a Victorian wrap-around shower, seeking out a days-gone-by approach to wash-a-day rigor will help you remain rooted in everyday things. Bring in your shaving cup and razor, find some good magazines, and leave the phone on the bureau.

Utility in the washroom can be well served by found treasures. It is one of the prime locations to display and use found hardware. Vintage hooks, accordion mirrors, medical cabinets and carts, metal baskets, and mason jars all work together in a graceful way. The inherent beauty and soft tones of even mass-produced soaps and tissues are made apparent when properly displayed.

Clean living. A bead-board wall is the perfect backdrop for a sunny bath. Clean towels hang readily from a hotel-style rack. A salvaged French door is curtained for privacy. Utility becomes art: freestanding shower handles take on the appearance of elegant sculpture, and promise relaxation.

People spend a good deal of time in the washroom, and tend to reflect there. Find things that make you feel happy and calm, and that force you to slow down. Editing is very important in this room. If a washroom is cluttered, it's hard think clearly; it might mean that the rest of the house—and perhaps one's life—is a bit cluttered as well. Simplicity serves both a functional and spiritual purpose in the washroom. Meditate on the small and beautiful details of this space, and you'll find that deep breathing comes a bit easier.

Found utility. This salvaged sink presents itself as a sturdy and reliable washup en route to the kitchen. A vintage mirror, galvanized tub, and wicker wastebasket help maintain a clean presence. Varying from a culture of predominantly white soaps, this blue bar gives a nice spot of color in its clean white surroundings.

A good boost. In the clean-lined serenity of this bath, a small Eames chair adds cool shape and warm color. A build-out keeps clutter at bay, complete with found mirrors for both dad and mom. A medical cart holds only the necessities for a quick shower in the Victorian-styled wrap-around. It was purchased as a discontinued floor sample from a plumbing supplier and patiently reassembled at home (sans instructions). With the addition of marble floors, this bath takes on the appearance of an early-twentieth-century spa while maintaining a modern view of practicality.

Grace in the everyday. A hospital medical cart is the perfectly sized caddy for shower and bath time. A vintage shaving mug comes out of retirement, and an aluminum soap carrier now acts as a temporary holder for jewelry and watches. Soap stored in a giant vintage clasp jar and tissue kept at hand with the help of a wire basket are small gestures that reveal an easy attitude. Beautiful milk glass that once held facial creams now holds hairpins and barrettes.

Small problems solved

Men's room. In this glass-tiled mini bath, art deco finishes are glorified with the addition of black-framed prints of business meetings and army camps. Good form is followed by good humor with the addition of a small souvenir marlin resting on top of cast pottery. Metal and glass containers keep things tidy.

The predicament that most people run into with small baths isn't necessarily the utility of space, but the clutter that collects with personal care products. In this small bath, found containers offer the solution to keeping the chaos in line. Instead of filling the walls with shelving that will only bring attention to your personal items, look for interesting boxes, baskets, and pottery to store your things away. Keep in mind the style of your space, and maintain a consistency of color and form, so that even when multiple bins are stacked or clustered, the room won't appear messy.

Bathroom scale. Large windows and hexagonal tile floors allow for many liberties in this vintage bath, already equipped with period hardware. The owners turned their attention to details, providing a glass-top metal end table, an old urn, an unfinished wooden chair, and a slip-covered ottoman, perfect for bath-side reading. Other details include a marble-top cabinet that holds an old aluminum lunch box keeping bath products together. A blue mason jar full of sea holly adds color and texture. A flea market portrait brings a calm, smiling face into the room.

Smart retreat. The large scale and open space of this bathroom is due to the fact that it was converted sometime around the turn of the nineteenth century (as indicated by the plumbing fixtures, sink and bathtub style). Now, with a few simple found additions, it has become the perfect retreat and private day spa. With easy-to-move furnishings, it allows for occasional yoga, meditation, and even exercise. A retracting slat bench usually reserved for gardening sits in the middle of the room to accept towels, candles, and perhaps tea. Salvaged finials and Chinese lanterns give a modern, free-spirited character to the space. An old, green-wicker hamper holds clean towels, and a stack of old books keeps the privy a bit more private.

141.

Washing day. An old laundry cart doubles as a rolling book cart and portrait prop. Wooden clothespins serve their true purpose in drying delicates from a retractable line. All the vintage sink needs is a small print referencing glorious water sources of lore. A butterbur leaf as grand and elegant as the space might provide quick cover-up if someone mistakes the large bathroom for a library.

CHAPTER 6

NATURAL HABITATS

The process by which most of us garden is the pure form of found style. Our outdoor spaces tend to be culminations of dozens or hundreds of trips to various garden centers over the course of several years in order to find the perfect flora, the best shrubbery, the most prized vegetables. We rummage through nurseries, greenhouses, discount centers, mail-order catalogs, and even flea markets for the right combination of plants, furniture, pottery, and decorative elements.

The difficulty of garden design is in wanting new gardens to look old and established. With found style, you can begin to add that look immediately. Vintage lawn furniture, handmade fabric pillows, and rustic urns all lend heritage to a garden on the rise. Architectural salvage is a great way to give age, interest, and structure to the garden as well. Anything from old iron fencing to stone building details set among the beds can add texture and backdrop to your plantings.

Found materials can be used to establish different moods within the garden area. Vintage Adirondack chairs set on a lawn under shady pines provide a respite from play, whereas mid-century metal chairs and a table set with vintage fabrics call out for high tea or a bottle of white wine. The repetitive use of old urns can create a formal backbone for gardens to grow within, while odd groupings of stone can make for interesting "canvases" for floral designs.

Found style can come from the garden as well. Decorating interiors with garden castoffs is a good way to bring in the feel of the outdoors. It's easy to be inspired by a simple bent

Pretty organized. A hand-crafted potting bench tucked under the exterior stairs becomes an inviting and cool spot to organize tools and planters. Architectural salvage, a small medicine cabinet, and plenty of galvanized buckets act as catchalls for a busy gardener. A flea market chandelier dripping with found crystal beads (like morning dew) might well be consumed by the greenery.

twig or stunning ocher leaf as well. Garden finds and weathered salvage brought indoors lend a feeling of casual grace to formal settings, and make for great conversation starters. Using salvage pottery and urns indoors to house your topiary, bulb forcings, and flowers is another great way to establish a natural and artistic flavor to any decor style. The very nature of the well-worn vessel transcends any design vocabulary, and will look right at home among your found style. Accenting our indoor surroundings with the beautiful forms found in nature helps us to keep a sense of our place in it. Nature educates us, astounds us, and removes us from our man-made cocoons to see the larger habitat we all share.

Mingling with greenery. A metal post cap and salvaged stone placed in the garden allow us to take a closer look at the amazing craft and detail that long ago might have disappeared into the fold of a much larger building. A teak table holds zinc pots of echeveria encircling a vintage sculpture in cast cement. The cool, silvery hues reflect the subtlety of the petunias behind.

Summer respite. Vintage wicker updated with new fabric and stainless-steel medical carts to hold books and whatnot rest well together on this stone porch. Vintage sconces and tall plant-display stands hold candles for evening, while hydrangeas, awaiting cooler days for planting, sit in vintage and new galvanized buckets for show. Just outside the porch, cupola finials collected over the years stand in a row so that we might pay tribute to their sculptured form from a bird's-eye view.

149.

Outdoor living. Dining alfresco is made more elegant with candles in antique metal holders, which provide romantic lighting for feasting around the simple farm table with a galvanized top. The rolling steel cabinet by the door is well suited as a summer catchall. The vintage chemistry beaker stand holds cuttings from larger bouquets, as well as a few old bell cloches, garden inspirations, and seed-gathering supplies.

Gathering place. This large cedar dining table is the centerpiece for all summer get-togethers. It rests on a sandstone platform porch built by the owner. A flea market chandelier hangs from a pulley some twenty feet above the table, and a *Queen Mary* deck chair remains the coveted seat in the back corner. Small glass balls are leftover cuttings from blown-glass globes; like oversized raindrops, they act as paperweights to hold down blow-away napkins during casual garden parties.

Curious details

A bit of copper tubing disappears below deck to hide the workings of this out-door washstand: a garden hose hooks up out of sight, making for easy winter disassembly and storage. The drain merely shoots runoff water out the back, so the entire unit can be stored inside. An early-twentieth-century flower stand affords close-up inspection of the miniature boxwood and evergreens displayed at eye level. The wisteria arch behind makes an inviting entrance to the patio area. Small cold frames made of vintage windows, rehinged at the top, create the perfect environment for early starts. A dramatic chandelier hangs high above the table from a pulley system rigged on a tree branch for ease of candle lighting.

Floral fabrics. This outdoor seating area is composed entirely of found furniture made cool and inviting with the help of a little repainting and the addition of vintage fabrics and pillows. A willow fence, small salvaged benches, and stone borders surround this shady retreat. The different styles of garden furniture are unified in their colors and in the way the fabric details are treated. A collection of artistic stone finials takes on the appearance of prize mushrooms in the gravel embankment of the hosta beds.

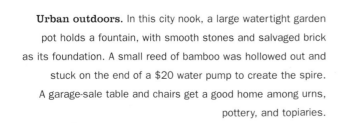

Urban outdoors. In this city nook, a large watertight garden pot holds a fountain, with smooth stones and salvaged brick as its foundation. A small reed of bamboo was hollowed out and stuck on the end of a $20 water pump to create the spire. A garage-sale table and chairs get a good home among urns, pottery, and topiaries.

Farmer's lunch. Under wisteria vines, the feeling of a grape orchard is captured with the help of simple country furnishings in painted wood. What may seem like Provence is really the Midwest with a little imagination and charm. After a day of hunting down found style, the owner's vintage International Scout is safe at home in the gravel drive just a stone's throw from the arbor. A tarnished, vintage silver-plated tray adds an elegant touch with its display of handmade candles.

161.

A not-so-muddy mud room. This utility space is made elegant through its well-edited collection of industrial ware. The heavy metal table with a wooden top, once used in light industry, is sturdy enough to use for potting but small enough to move for increased floor space when needed. Jute rugs protect the wood floors from pottery and bags of soil, while a science-lab stool seems appropriate to the methodical task at hand. A vintage mirror holds a small garden inspiration. Plant markers and pencils await use in a ceramic eggcup, and an old ironstone pitcher now serves as a gentle watering can.

Sorting in style. Showing us that even the smallest of tasks can be performed with the grace and utility of great found style, everlasting seeds are gathered and sorted on enamel industrial trays before being stored and marked. An old sieve acts as perfect holding tank for stems not yet stripped, and wild fennel pods await storage in ceramic salt dishes.

165.

Nature found. Oftentimes what we seek is literally right under our feet. Part of this gardener's space is the "nature center" of his hundred-acre farm. The potting/mud room itself becomes a living history museum and testament to the beauty inherent in natural forms. An old clip rack from a store holds natural wonders on postcards below the folk-art deer carving. A salvaged sideboard holds lovingly framed feathers, skins, bones, and nests.

Rural tribute. A wall of a potting porch holds vintage farm implements found on the property, framed pages from an old children's nature magazine, and mounted ducks. Found style is a state of mind; a row of stones brought from the beach reflect Zen-like simplicity in their careful arrangement.

EPILOGUE

FIND YOURS

Hopefully you've gained some inspiration from the creative homes in this book. And hopefully you're already on your way to discovering your own found style. Remember that the search itself is a creative process, and that the true reflection of "who you are" will always evolve depending on the whims and desires of your ever-changing voice. *—David and Amy Butler*

PROGRESS LUSTRANE   Art. 240
Col.   12 Yards

You can't find your style until you begin the hunt. But where do you start? A little research helps. It will also make your life easier to understand a little bit about the objects of your desire. So here is a starting point. The Internet is a fantastic tool for finding not only the objects of your desire, but discovering new ones. This list makes for a good road map, but do a little research on your own for local antique shops, flea markets, and shows. The best stories (and the best bargains) come with getting out there and digging for treasure.

GENERAL INFO ONLINE

The following sites will help you start your search offering great all-around information on shows, shops, and antique malls.

www.acguide.com
guide to finding antiques/shops

www.antiqueshopsa2z.com
guide to finding antiques/shops

www.antique-central.com
guide to finding antiques/shops

www.antiqueshopsusa.com
guide to finding antiques/shops

www.antiqueguide.net
guide to finding antiques/shops

www.brassarmadillo.com
guide to finding antique shops

www.collectingnetwork.com
guide to finding antiques and information

www.consignmentshops.com
guide to finding antique shops

www.europeantiques.net
antiques of all sorts - Europe

www.europebynet.com
antique shop finder - Europe

www.fleamarketguide.com
guide to finding show locations and dates

www.riverfront-antique.com
guide to finding antiques/shops

www.the-forum.com
guide to finding antiques/shops

www.tias.com
guide to finding antiques/shops

www.ultracollector.com
guide to finding antiques/shops

SHOWS

Here are some of the best regional flea markets in the United States

NORTHEAST AND MID ATLANTIC

THE ANNEX ANTIQUES FAIR & FLEA MARKET
New York, NY
212-243-5343
www.annexantiques.citysearch.com

BRIMFIELD
Brimfield, MA
413-283-6149
www.brimfieldshow.com

FARMINGTON ANTIQUES WEEKEND
Farmington, CT
317-598-0012
www.farmington-antiques.com

MULFORD FARM ANTIQUE SHOW AND SALE
Hampton, NY
631-537-0333

SHUPP'S GROVE
Adamstown, PA
717-484-4115
www.shuppsgrove.com

MIDWEST

CENTREVILLE ANTIQUES MARKET
Centreville, MI
773-227-4464

SANDWICH ANTIQUES MARKET
Sandwich, IL
773-227-4464

SCOTT ANTIQUE SHOW
Columbus, OH
740-569-2800
www.scottantiquemarket.com

SPRINGFIELD FLEA MARKET
Springfield, OH
937-325-0053
www.springfield-clarkcountyohio.info
/antique_show.htm

WEST

PORTLAND ANTIQUE SHOW
Portland, OR
503-282-0877
www.palmerwirfs.com

ROSE BOWL FLEA MARKET
PASADENA, CA
323-560-7469
www.rgcshows.com/rosebowl.asp

SANTA MONICA OUTDOOR ANTIQUE AND COLLECTIBLE MARKET
Santa Monica, CA
323-933-2511

SOUTH

HEART OF COUNTRY
Nashville, TN
800-862-1090
www.heartofcountry.com

KENTUCKY FLEA MARKET
Louisville, KY
502-456-2244
www.stewartpromotions.com

METROLINA EXPO FLEA MARKET
Charlotte, NC
919-596-4643

RENNINGER'S FLORIDA TWIN MARKET
Mt. Dora, FL
352-383-8393
www.renningers.com

ROUND TOP
Round Top, TX
281-493-5501
www.roundtopantiquesfair.com

SCOTT ANTIQUE SHOW
Atlanta, GA
740-569-2800
www.scottantiquemarket.com

ONLINE RETAILERS, CATALOGS, & SHOPPING

Here are some of our favorite sites offering a variety of found style for every room. Some of these offer online shopping or the ordering of specialty furnishings, others give information on store locations. Most of them do both.

www.abccarpet.com
212-473-3000
eclectic home furnishings & finishes

www.anthropologie.com
800-309-2500
vintage and reproduction antique furnishings

www.atomichome.com
20th century furnishings & antiques

www.budnbettys.com
antiques of all sorts - Canada

www.californiachair.com
20th century furnishings & antiques

www.circa1950.com
20th century furnishings & antiques - UK

www.design20thcentury.com
20th century furnishings & antiques - Australia

www.designandfun.com
20th century furnishings & antiques - Austria

www.dicksrestaurantsupply.com
800-294-7598
industrial restaurant supplier

www.dmk.dk
20th century furnishings & antiques - Denmark

www.dwr.com
800-944-2233
modern furnishings

www.economysupply.com
973-279-5500
industrial restaurant supplies

www.farrow-ball.com
traditional paints and wallpapers - UK

www.fearsandkahn.co.uk
20th century furnishings & antiques - UK

www.fishseddy.com
877-347-4733
vintage dinnerware & antiques

www.galley.com
985-868-9240
restaurant supply

www.hotproperty.ca
antiques of all sorts - Canada

www.knoll.com
877-61knoll
20th century furnishings & antiques

www.lauraashley.com
country modern furnishings - UK

www.leejofa.com
classic reproduction furnishings and fabrics - UK

www.luna-online.com
20th century furnishings & antiques - UK

www.lounge-design.nl
20th century furnishings & antiques - Netherlands

www.machine-age.com
617-482-0048
20th century furnishings & antiques

www.marcomodernariato.com
20th century furnishings & antiques - Italy

www.meritmetal.com
215-343-2500
vintage reproduction hardware

www.missionrestaurantsupply.com
800-254-5042
restaurant supply

www.modernica.net
212-219-1303
20th century furnishings & antiques

www.modernity.nu
20th century furnishings & antiques - Sweden

www.modernvintagefurniture.com
20th century furnishings & antiques

www.modnorthwest.com
20th century furnishings & antiques

www.modpad.tripod.com
20th century furnishings & antiques - UK

www.moebelarkitekten.dk
20th century furnishings & antiques - Denmark

www.monroesaltworks.com
888-525-4471
antiques of all sorts

www.ovalinteriors.com
20th century furnishings & antiques - UK

www.pottery.dk
20th century pottery - Denmark

www.predicta.com
vintage reproduction televisions

www.psmodernway.com
760-320-5455
20th century furnishings & antiques

www.reprodepot.com
vintage reproduction fabrics

www.restaurantsupplydepot.com
866-559-0555
restaurant supply

www.restorationhardware.com
800-762-1005
reproduction antique furnishings/hardware

www.retroathome.com
510-658-6600
20th century furnishings & antiques

www.retrodesign.free.fr
20th century furnishings & antiques - France

www.rubylane.com
antiques of all sorts

www.smeguk.com
vintage-style appliances - UK

www.smithandhawken.com
800-776-3336
garden supplies/antique reproduction garden wares

www.sonrisafurniture.com
20th century furnishings & antiques

www.swankarama.com
919-832-3030
20th century furnishings & antiques

www.tri-stateantiques.com
antiques of all sorts

www.watermonopoly.com
vintage reproduction bath fixtures - UK

www.xxo.com
20th century furnishings & antiques - France

www.zebramodernariato.com
20th century furnishings & antiques - France

www.zimmerdahl.se
20th century furnishings & antiques - Sweden

www.zitzo.com
20th century furnishings & antiques - Netherlands

ACKNOWLEDGMENTS
THANKS!

To the amazing folks who have contributed their time in the making of this book. Especially for allowing us to come into their homes and capture years of great found style in the making.

Brian and Nora Corbett

Keith and Monique Keegan

Paul and Amy Hamilton

Erwin and Christine Dauch-Weber

Kevin Reiner and Chuck Ross

Michael Rosen and Mark Svede

Robert Gorst and Dawn Sweitzer

Also, thanks to our favorite regional shops that we frequent, and provide us with a broad range of found style.

FARLEY & MOORE ANTIQUES LTD
104 South Main Street
Mount Vernon, OH 43050
740-392-4590

MEMORY LANE ANTIQUES
229 South Main Street
Mount Vernon, OH 43050
(740) 397-5664

SECOND TIME AROUND
120 West High Street
Mount Vernon, OH 43050
(740) 397-0848

ALEXANDER & RHODES
211 South Main Street
Mount Vernon, OH 43050
740-392-7070

SOBO STYLE
3129 N. High St.
Columbus, OH 43202
614-447-8880

Special thanks to Colin, Jennifer, and Anita for capturing the spirit of these creative ventures with such artistic vision, enthusiasm, and efficiency. Also Janet at Homewood Farms Greenhouse and Nursery, and Kevin at Timbuk Farms Nursery, for helping us to not only show, but identify, the found style plants in this book. And huge thanks to Mikyla, Ben, and Leslie at Chronicle Books for the patience, kindness, and exquisite guidance in the making of this book.